I0490226

COLORING BOOK

PUPPY

24 IMAGES WAITING FOR COLORATION

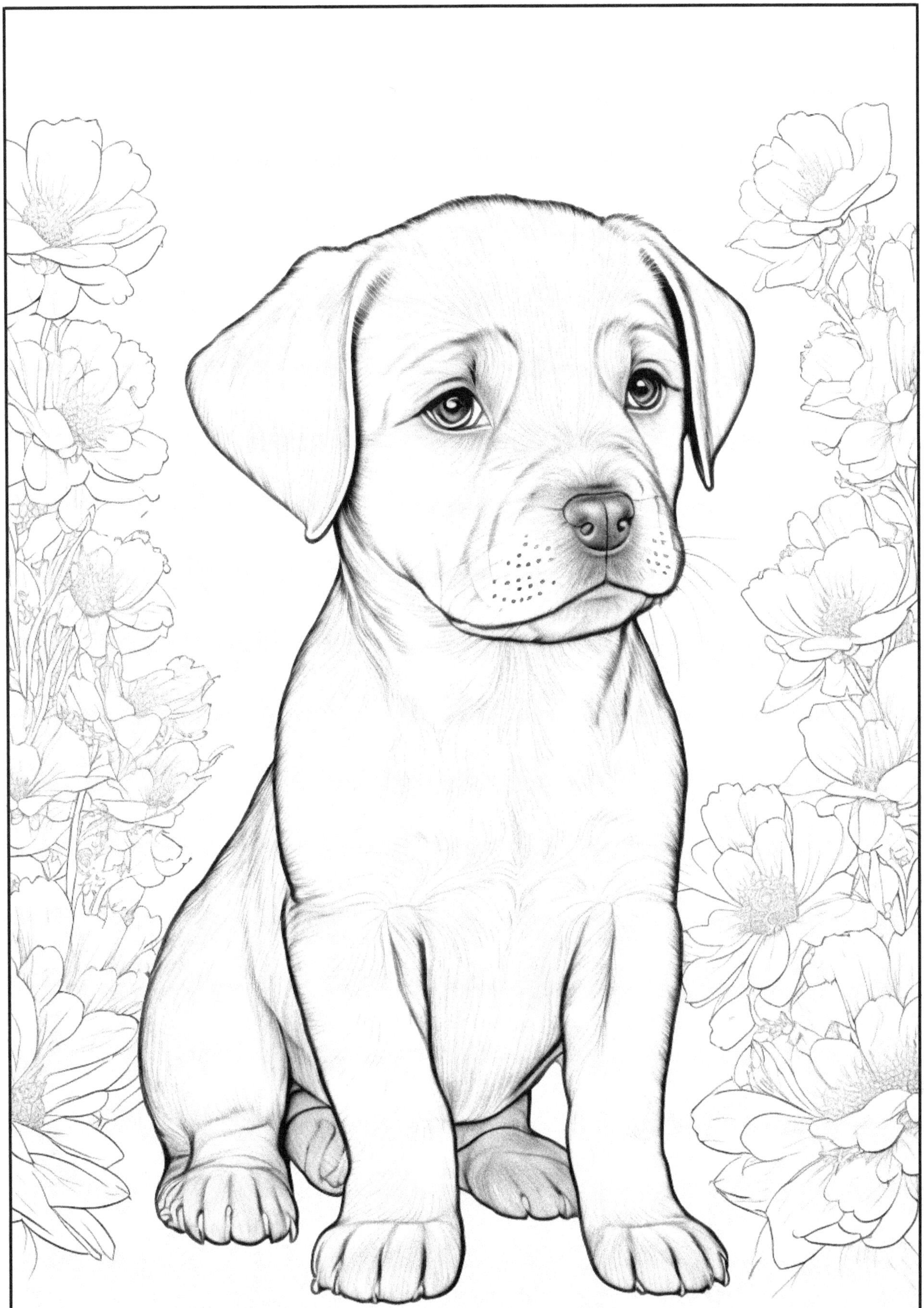

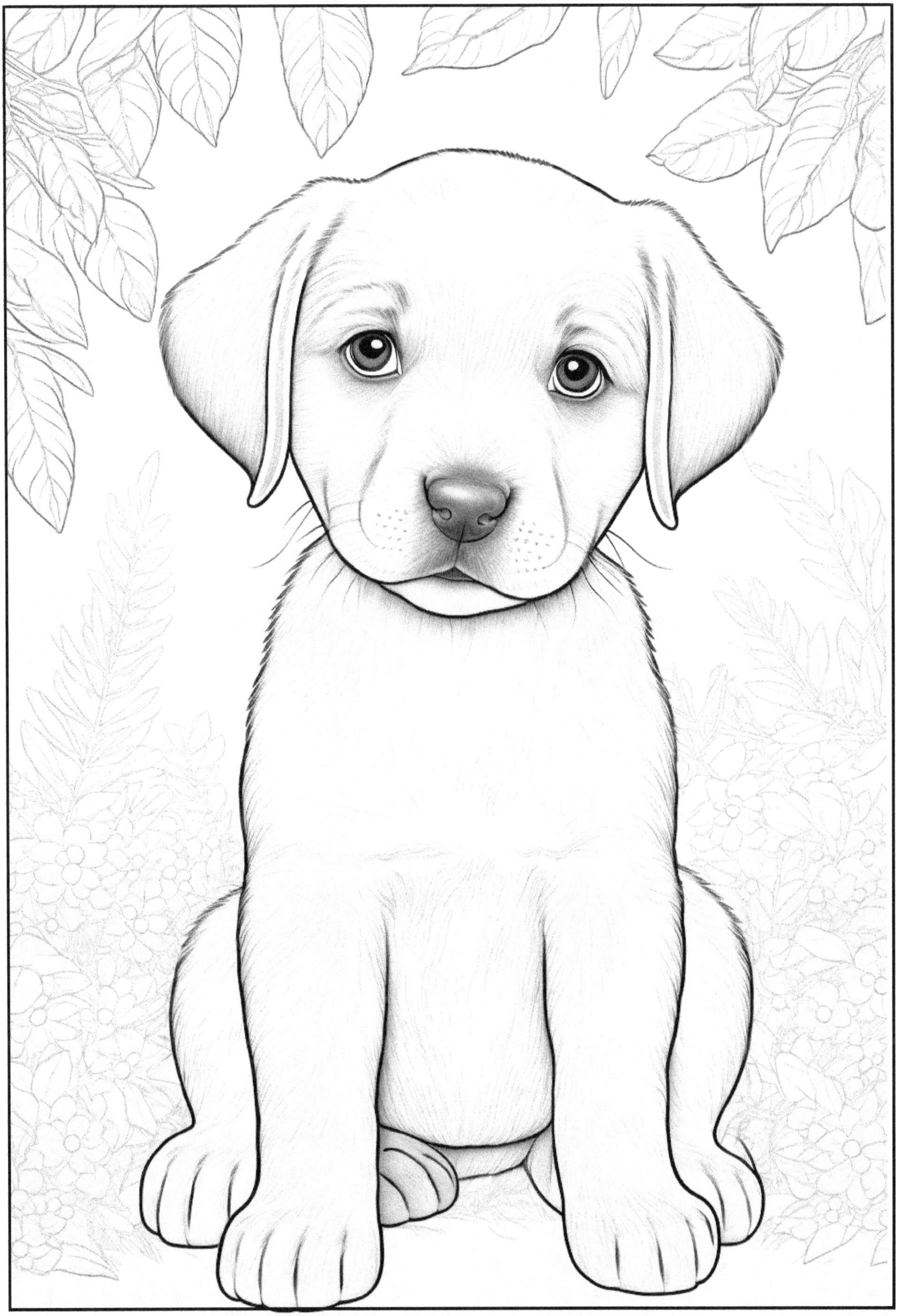

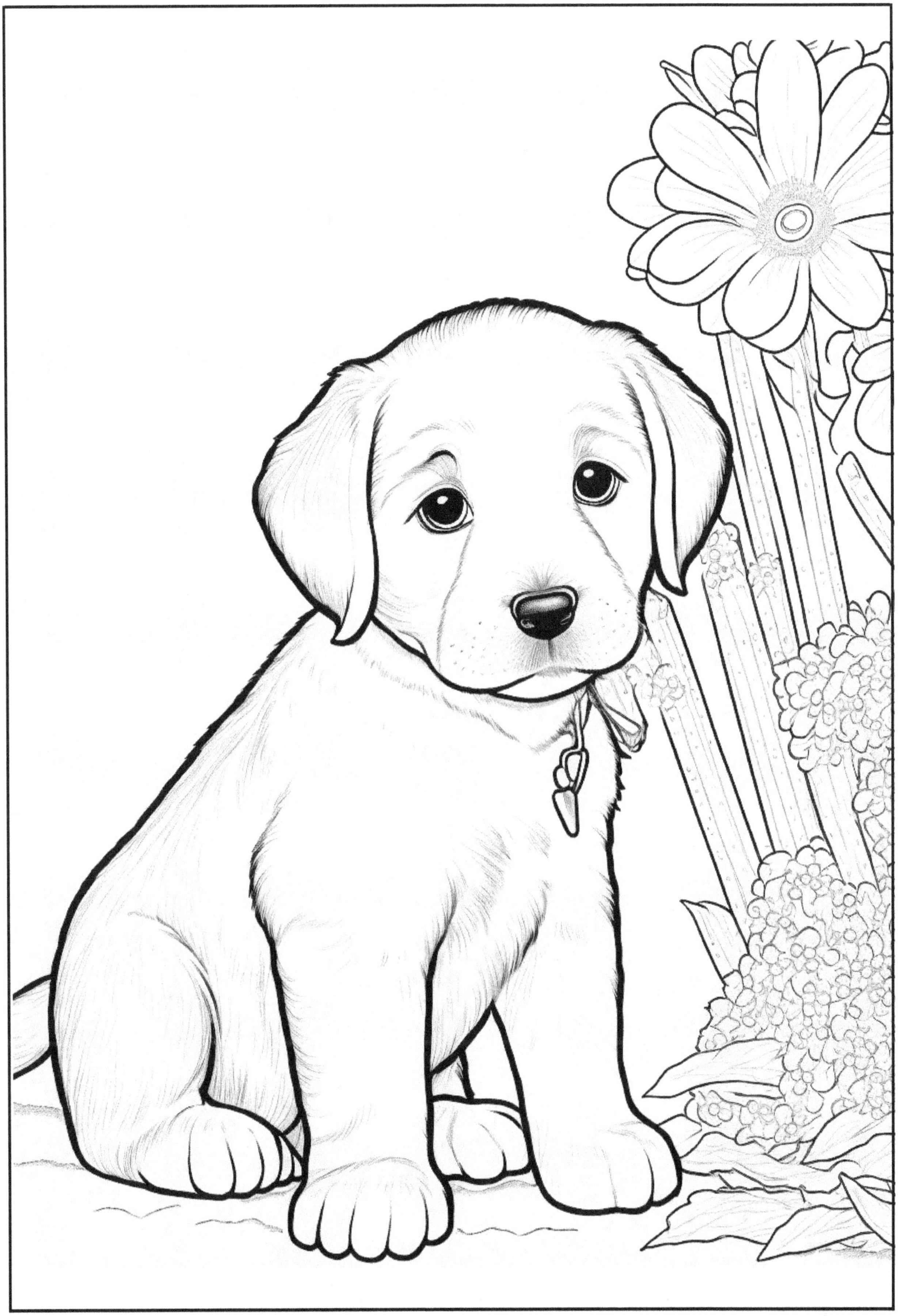

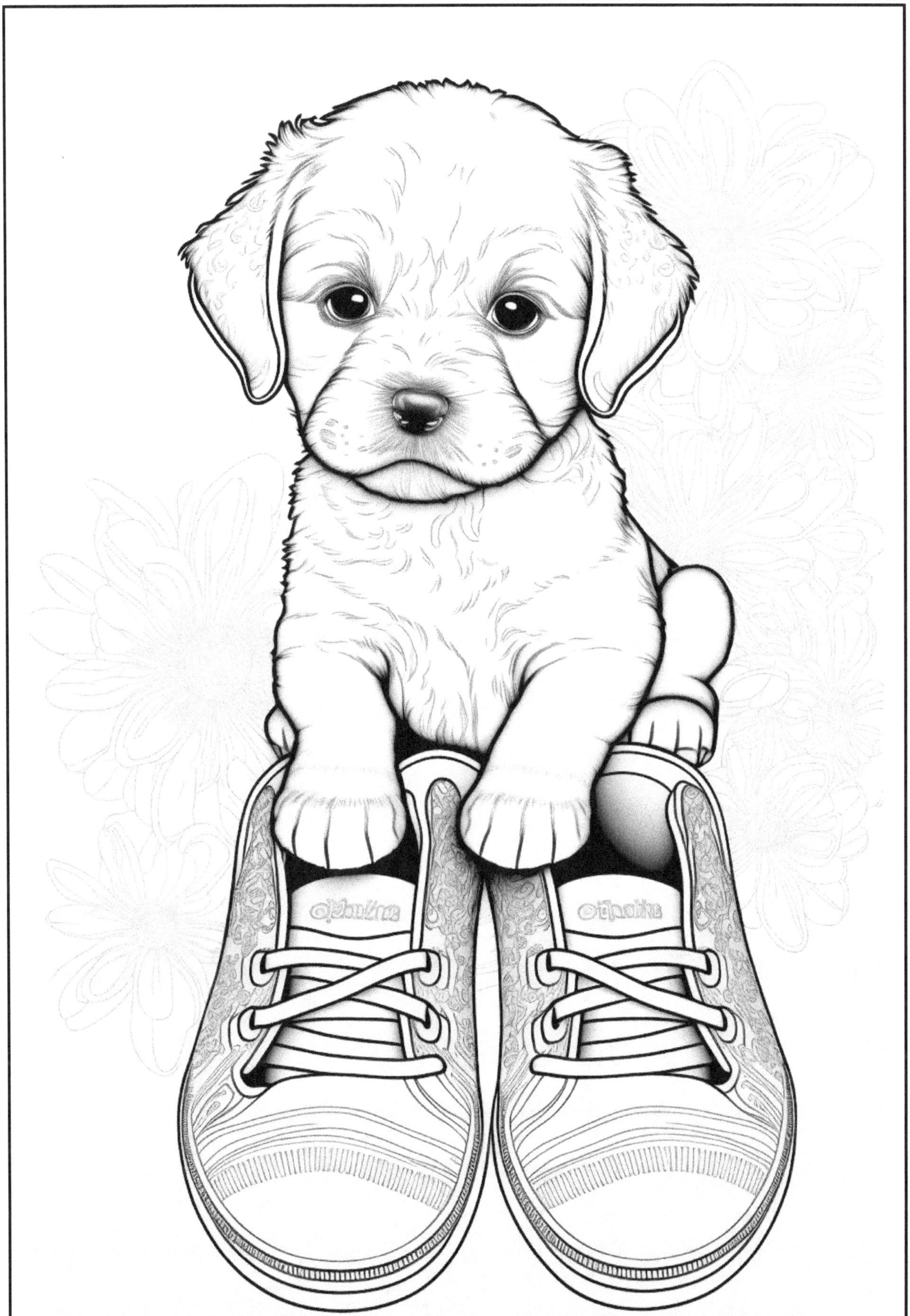

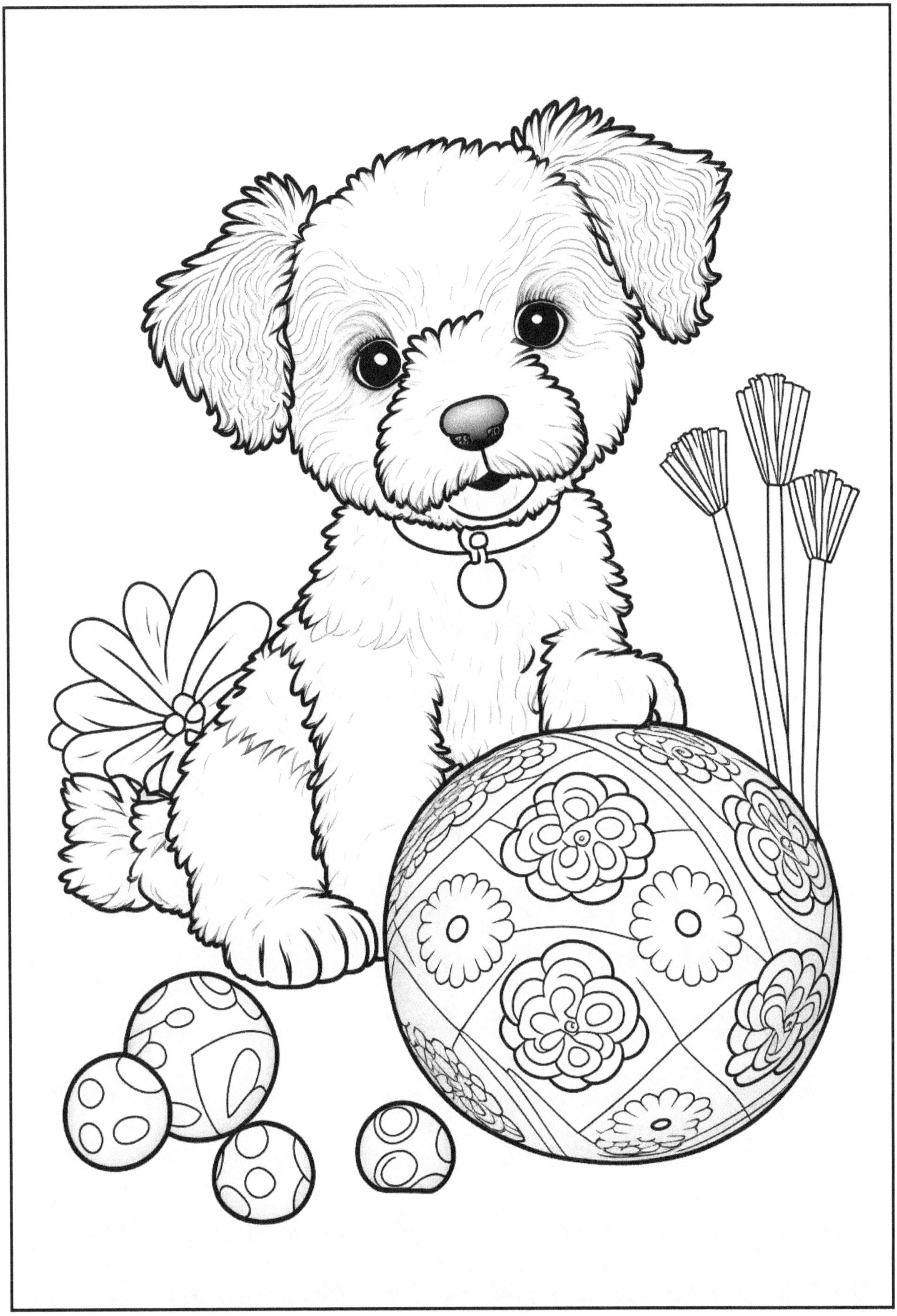

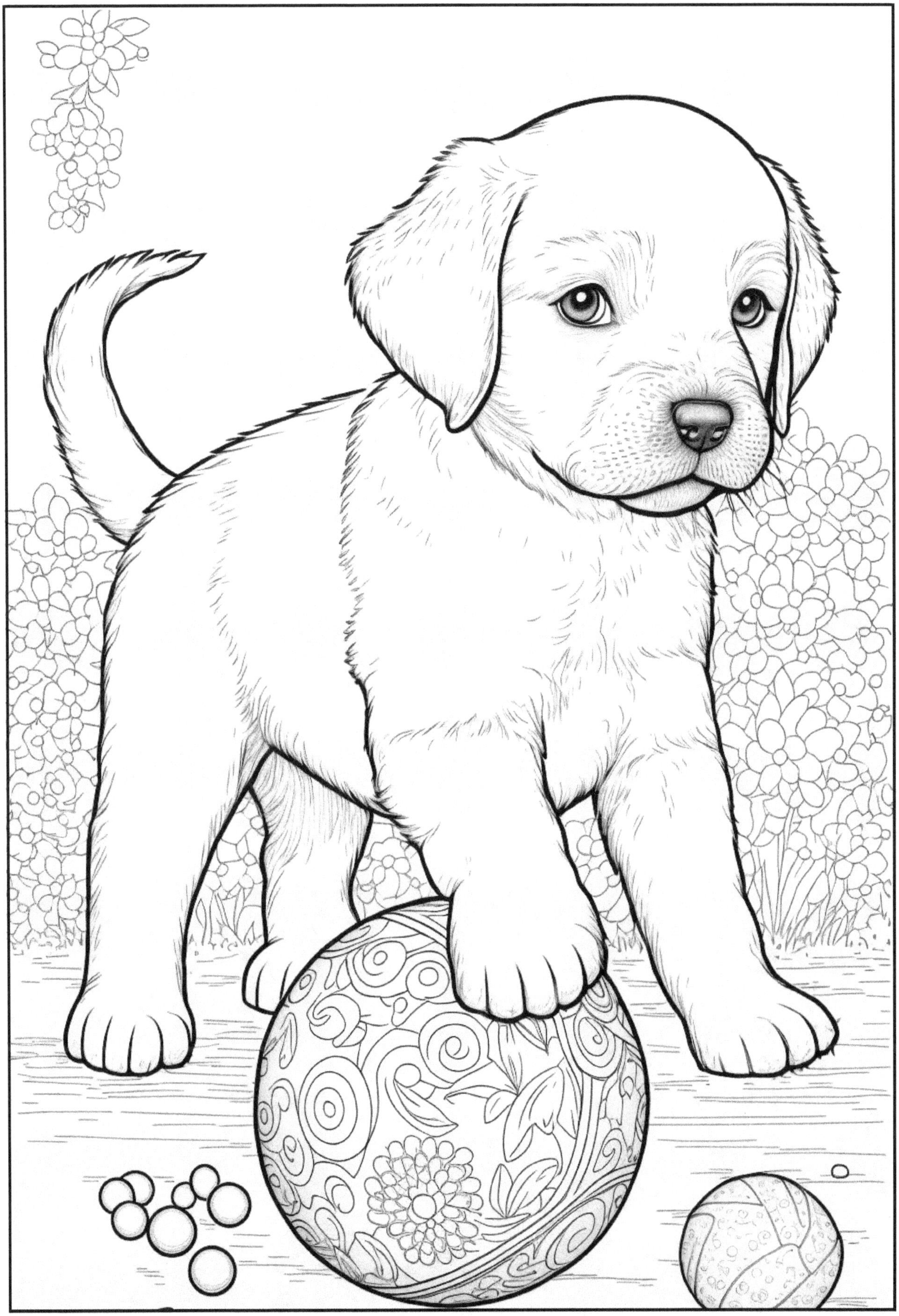

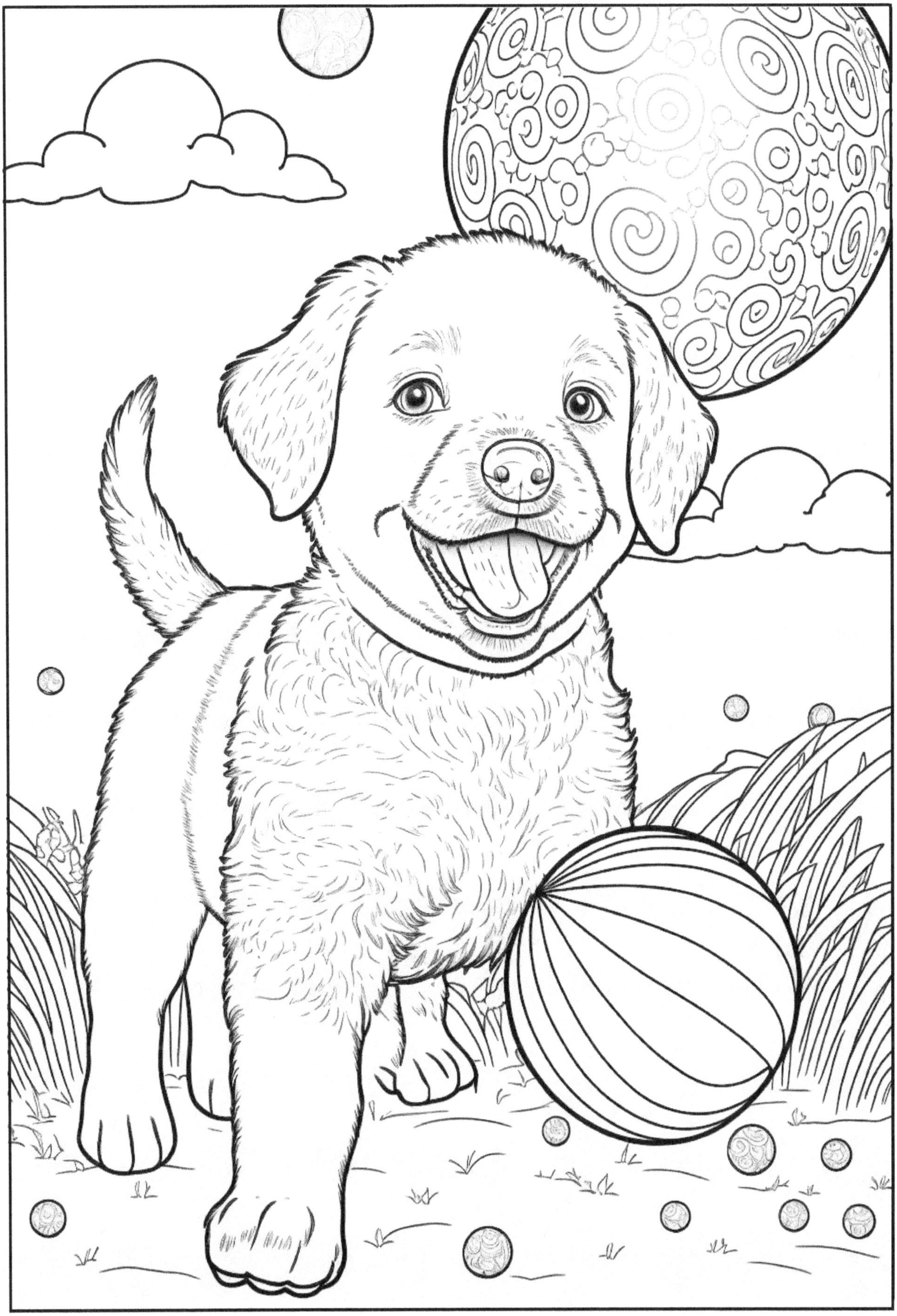

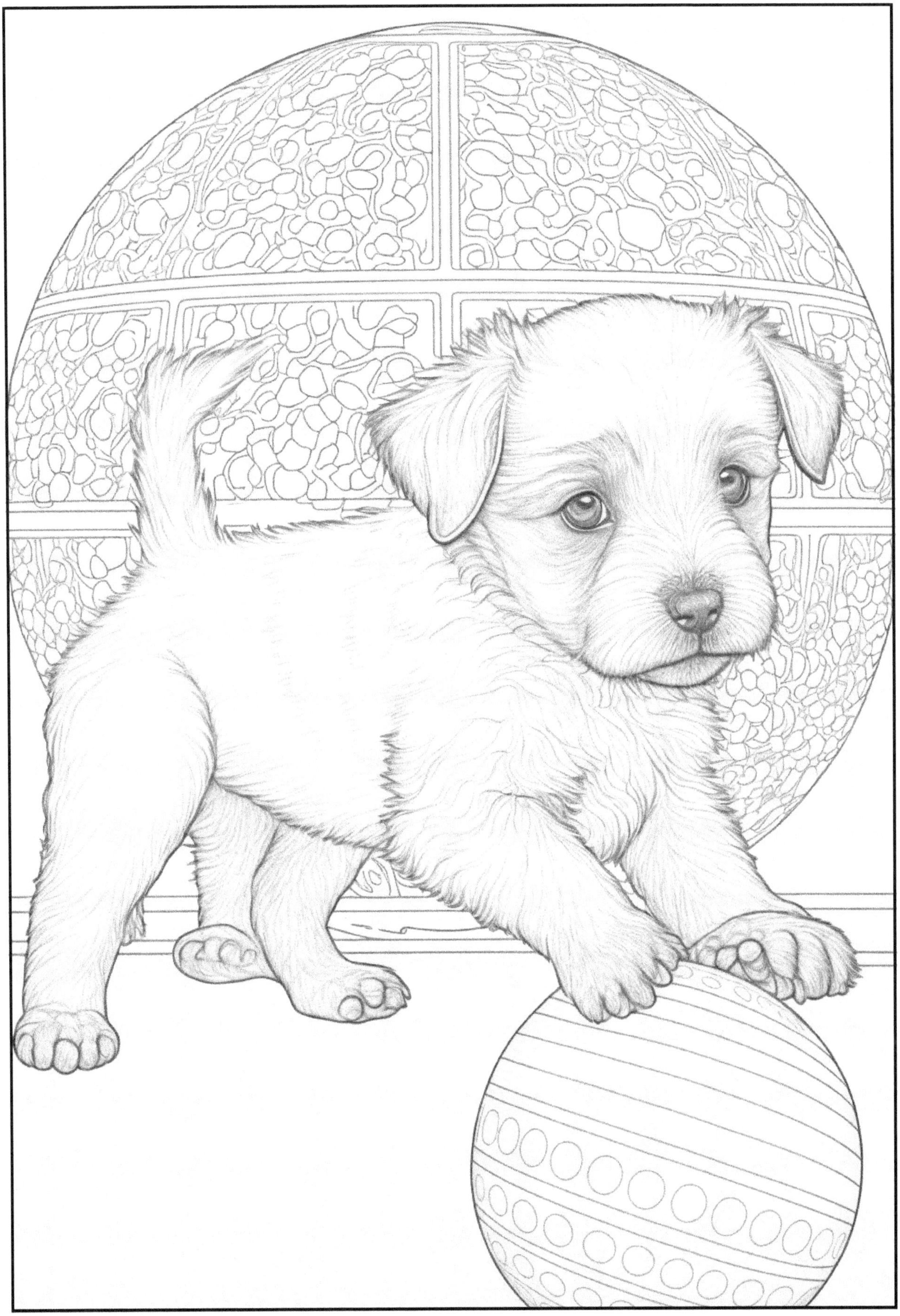

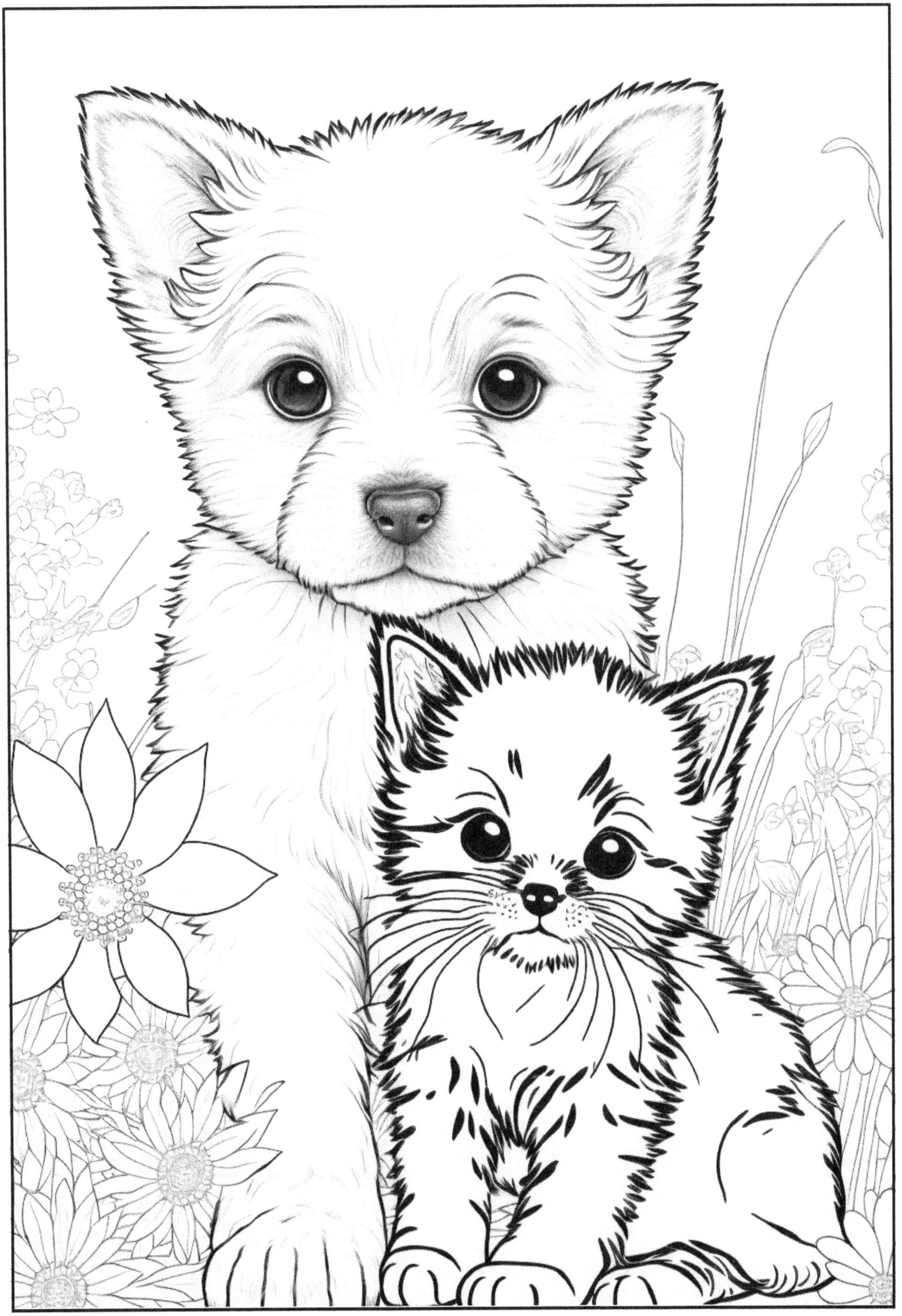

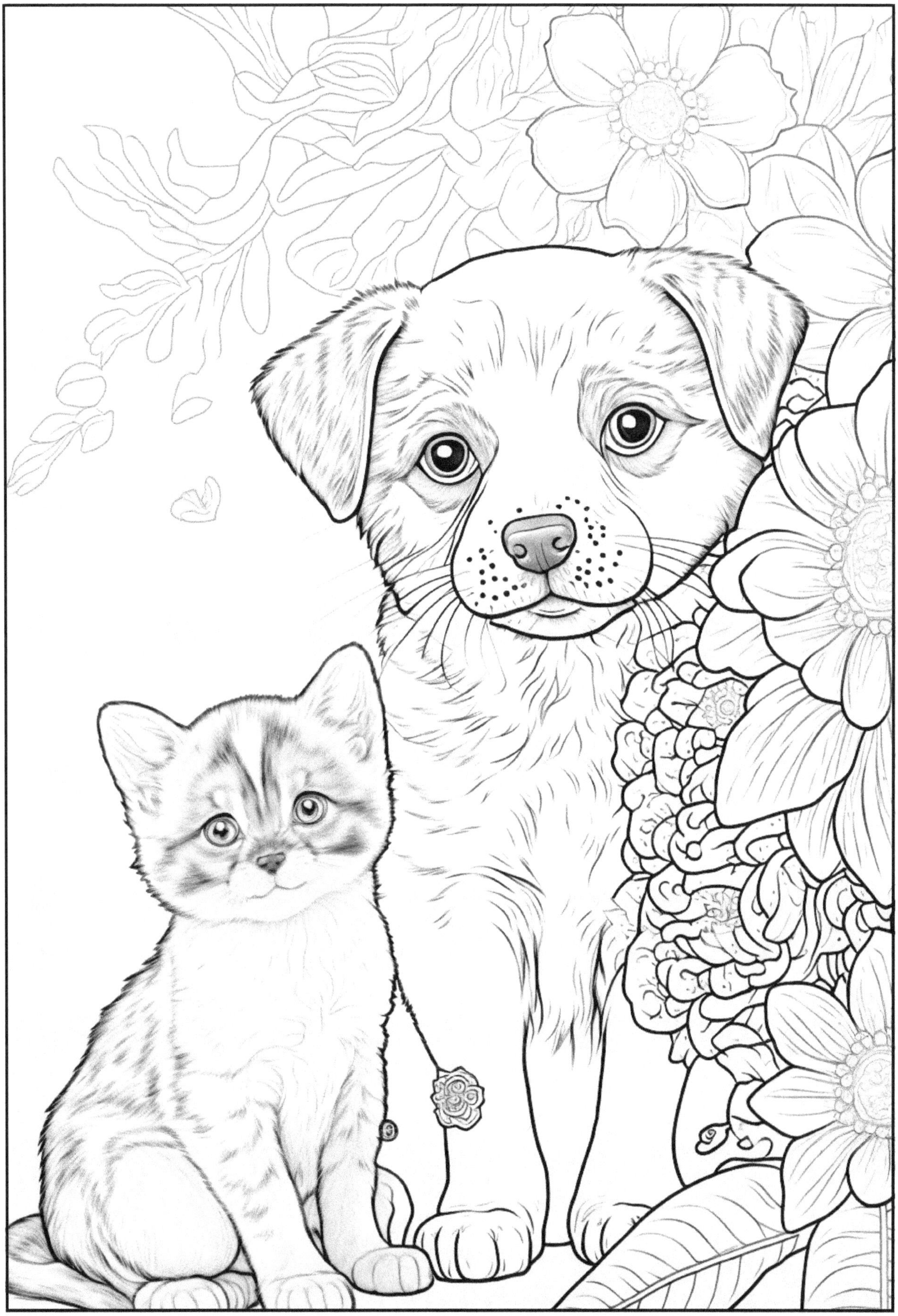

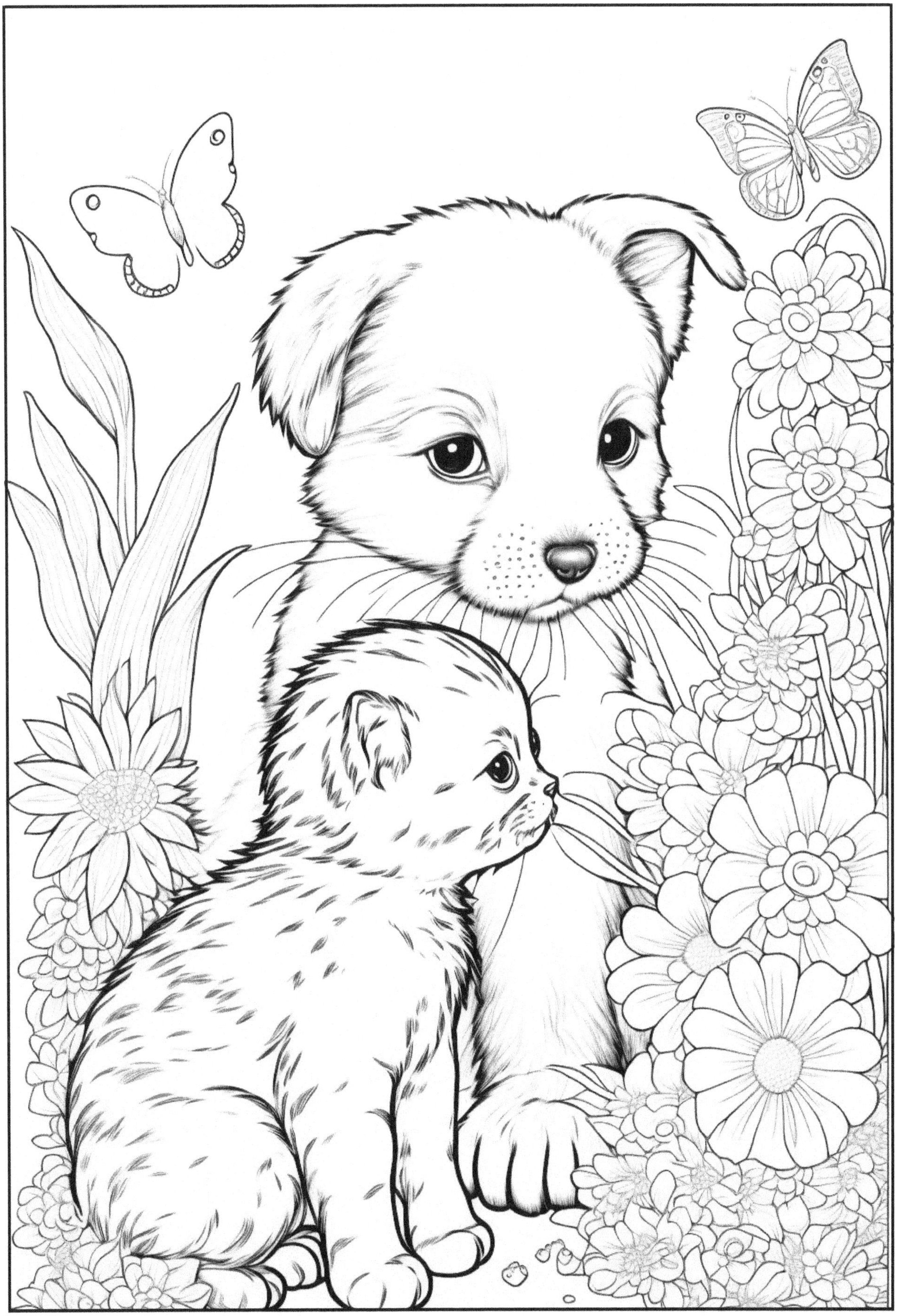

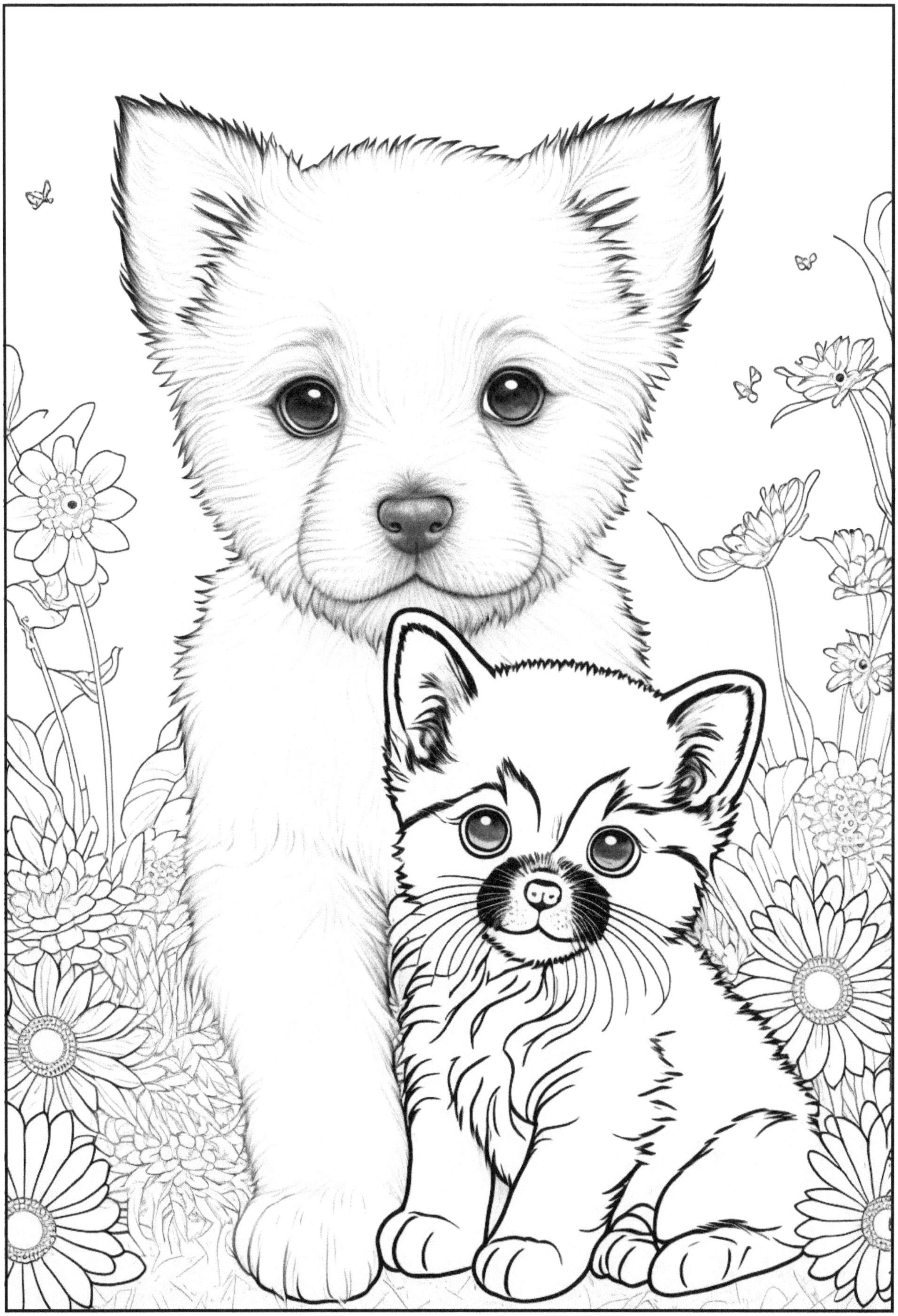

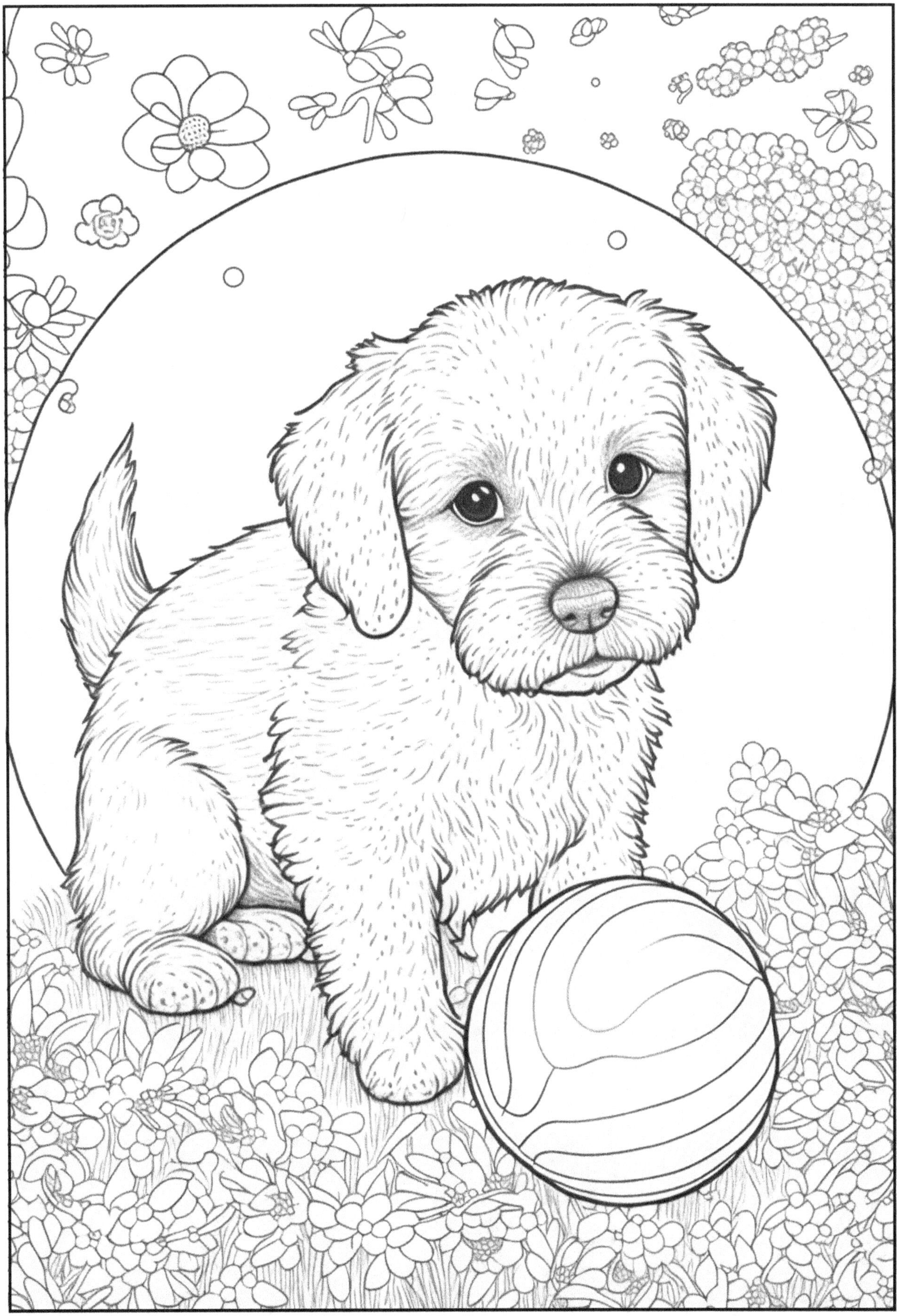

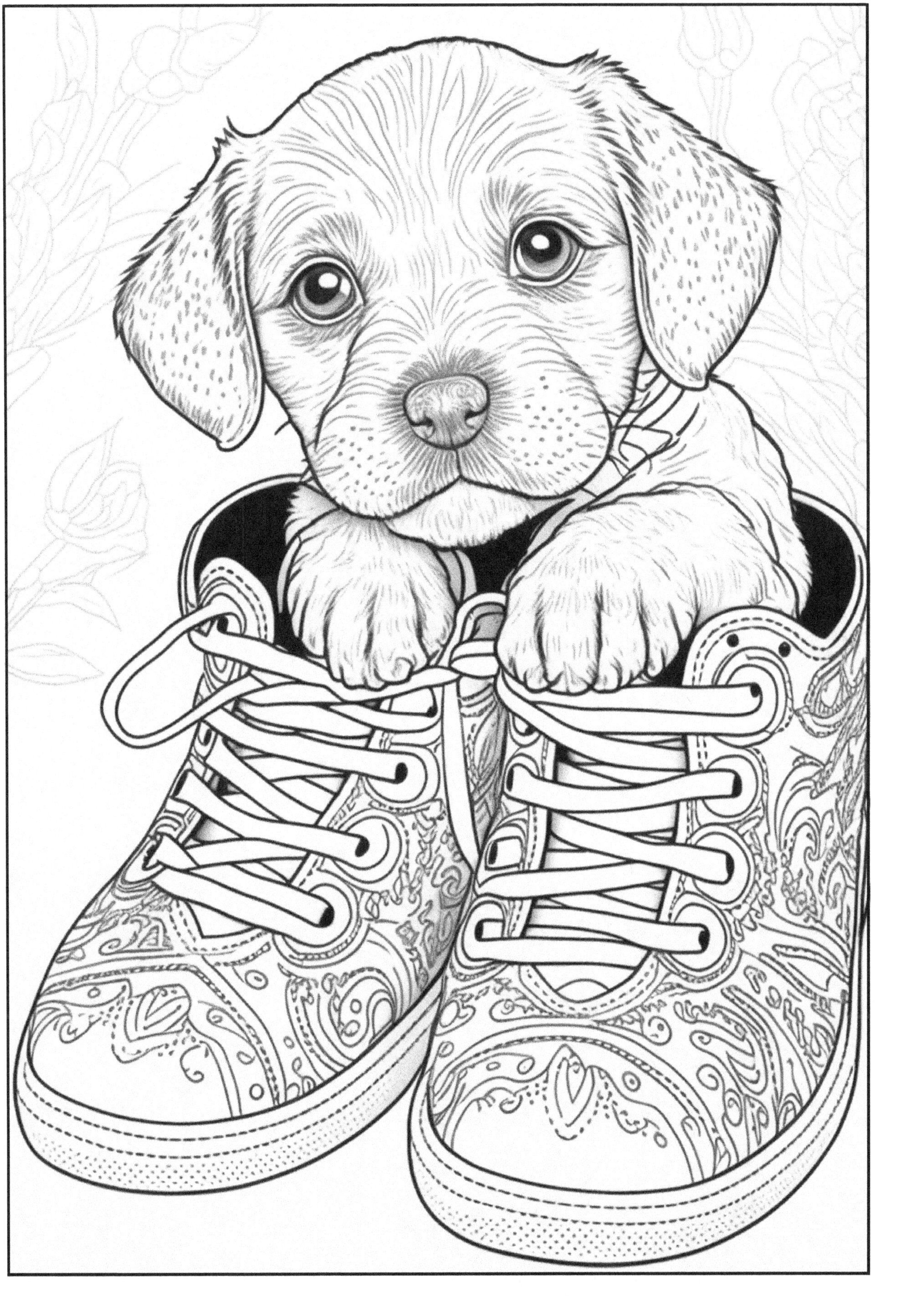

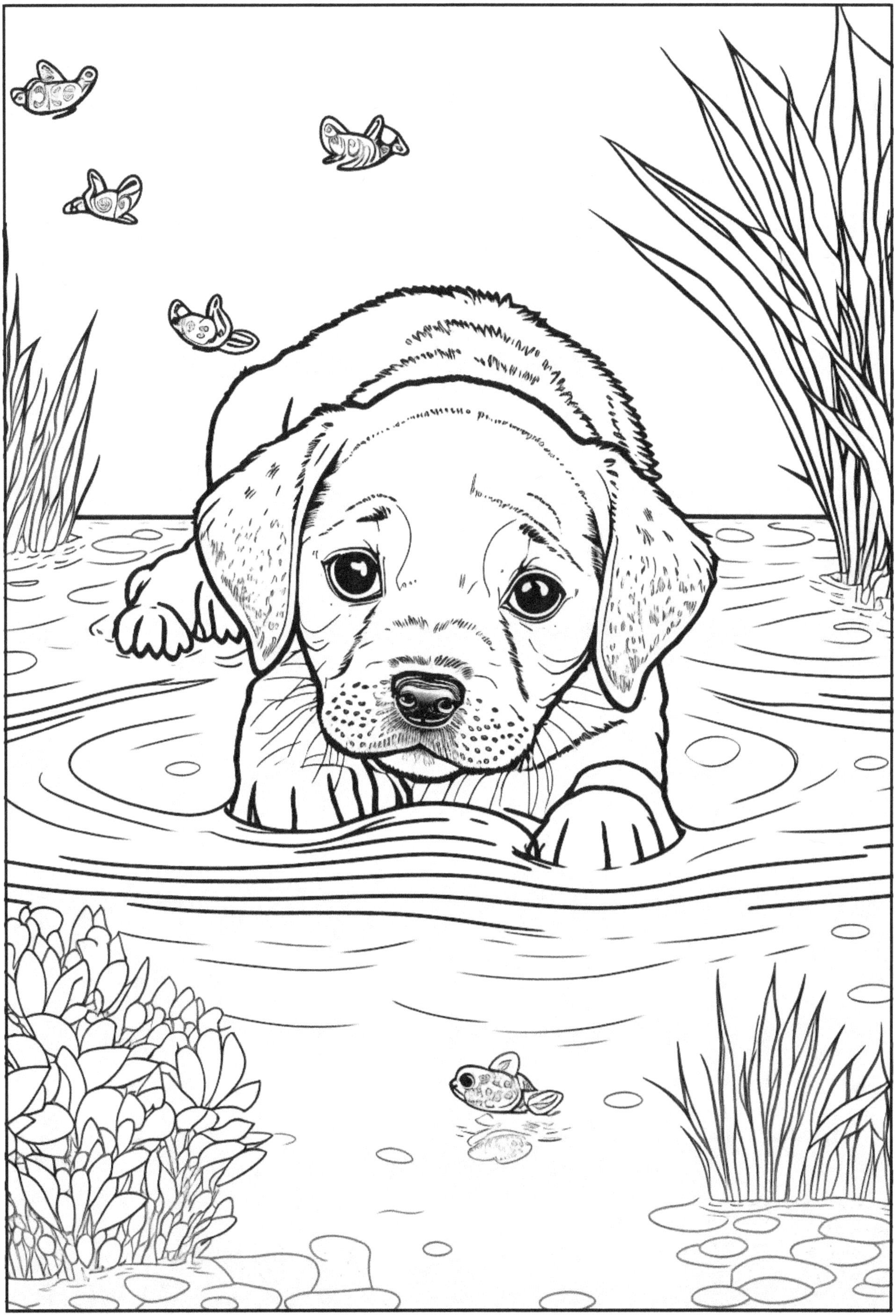

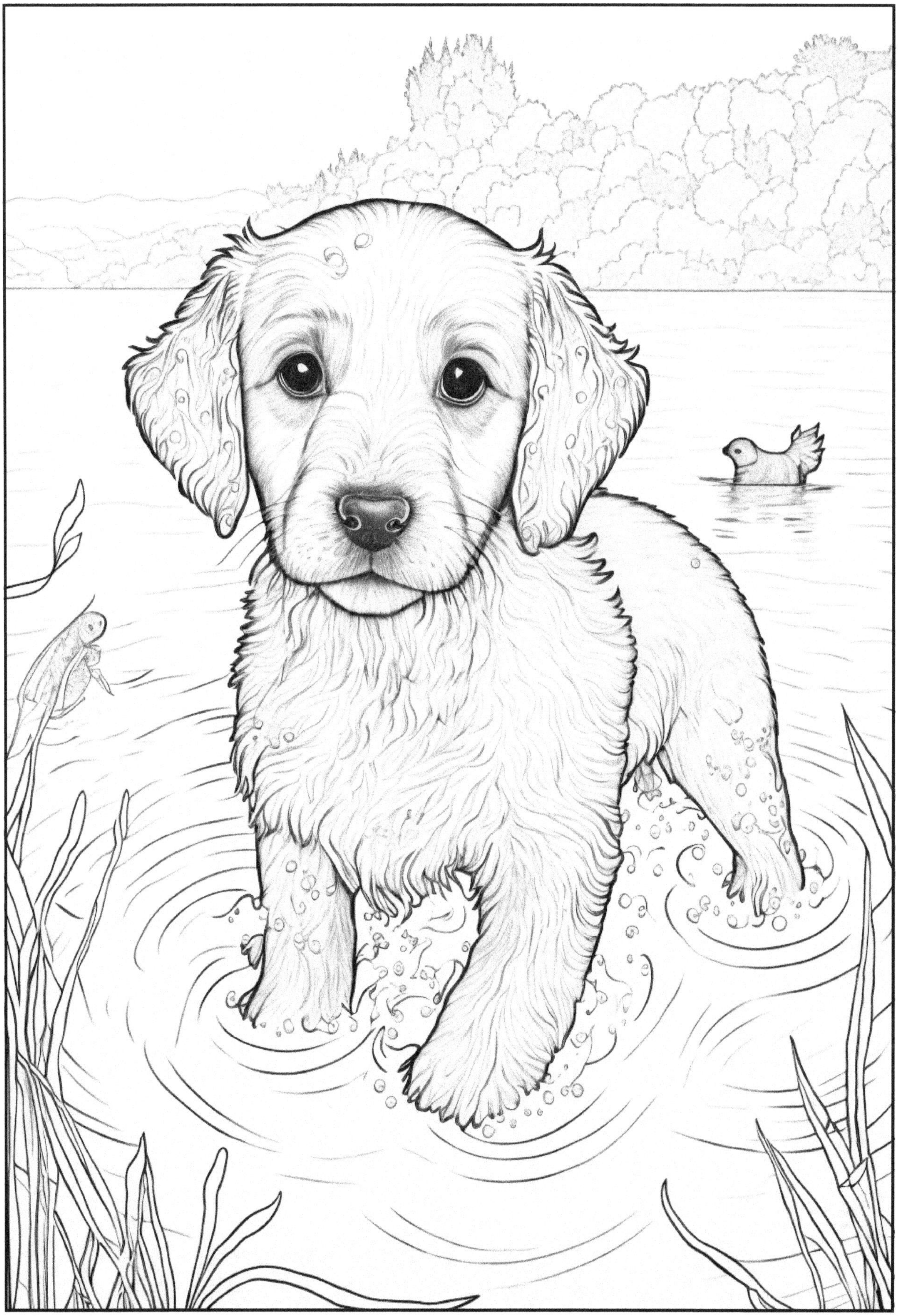

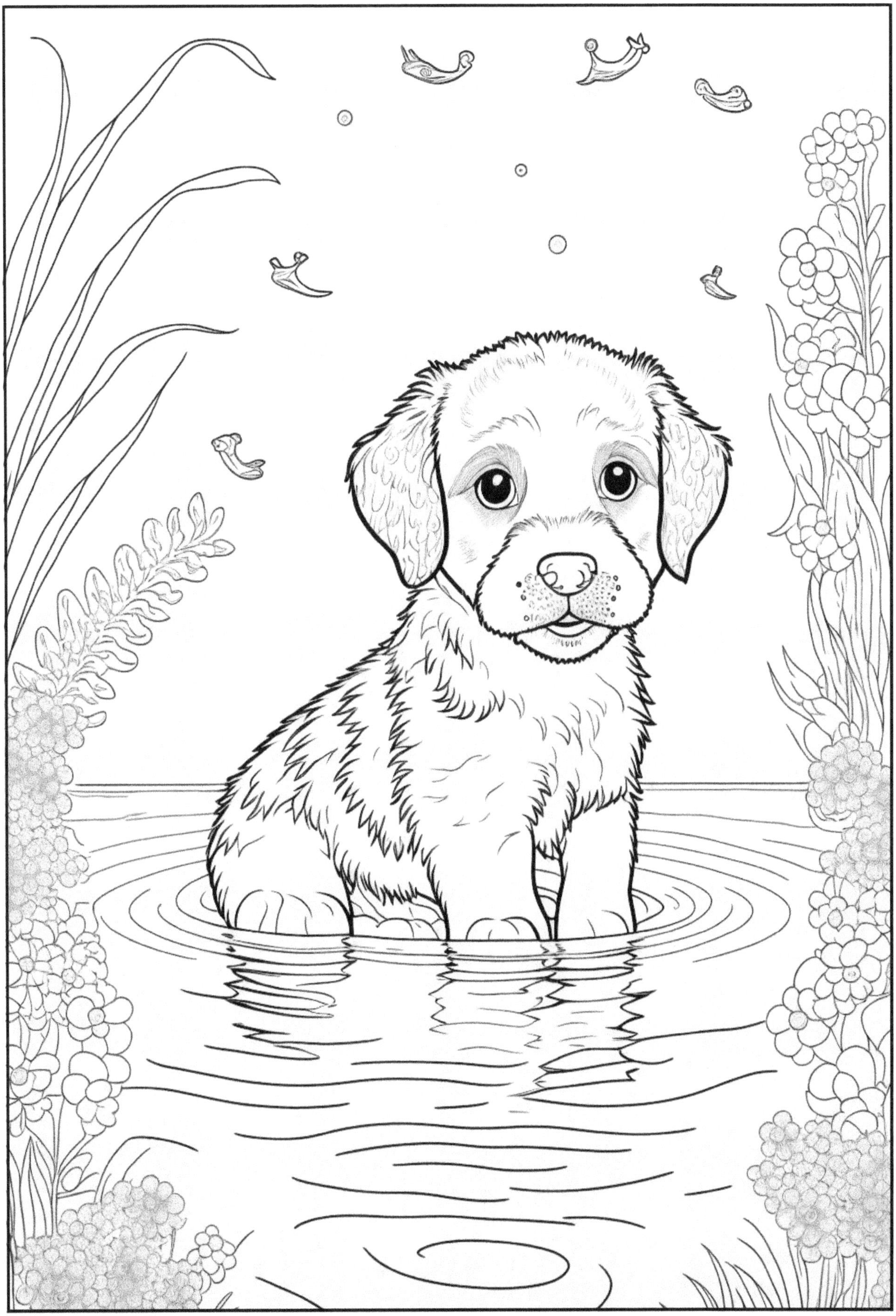

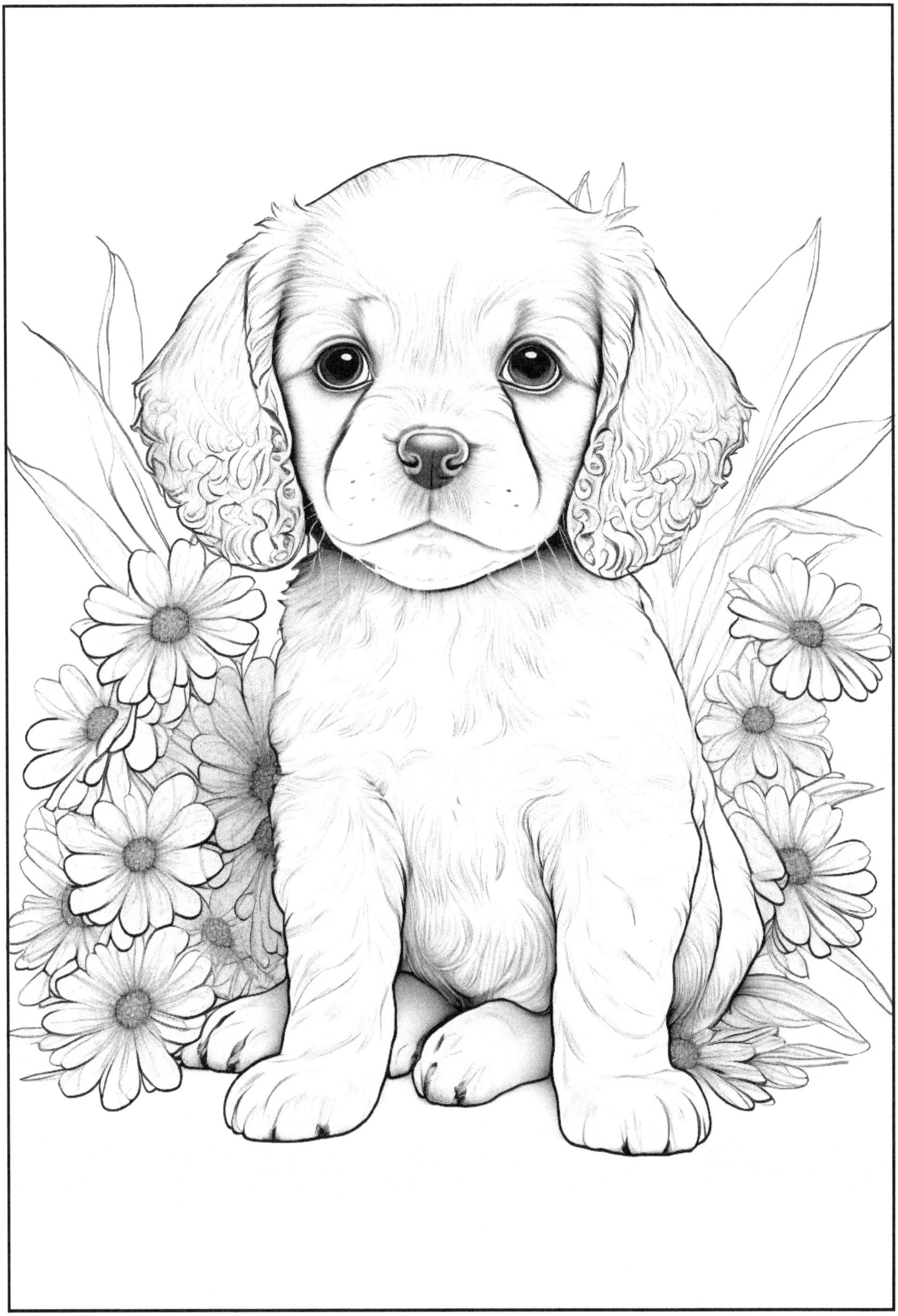

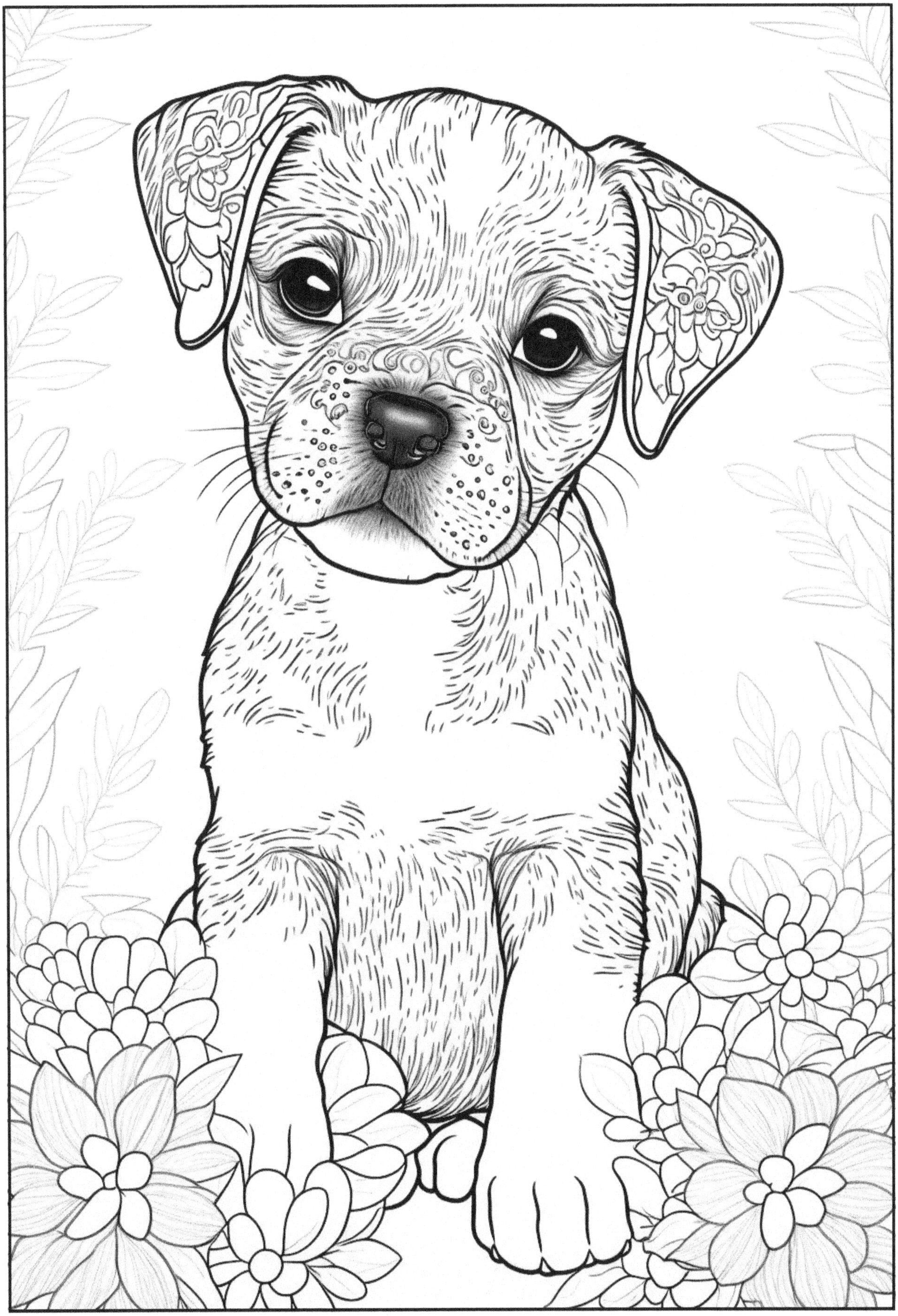

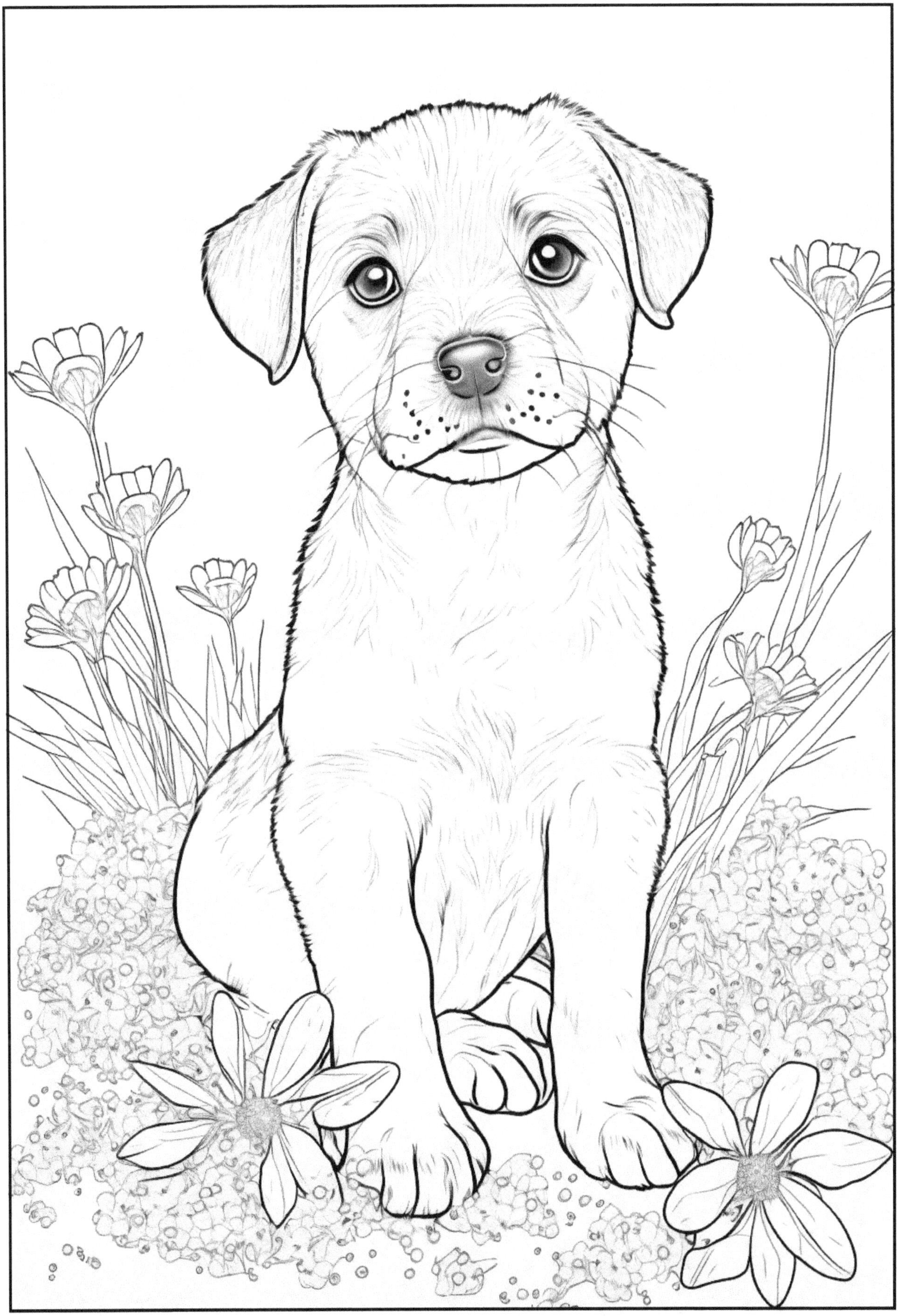

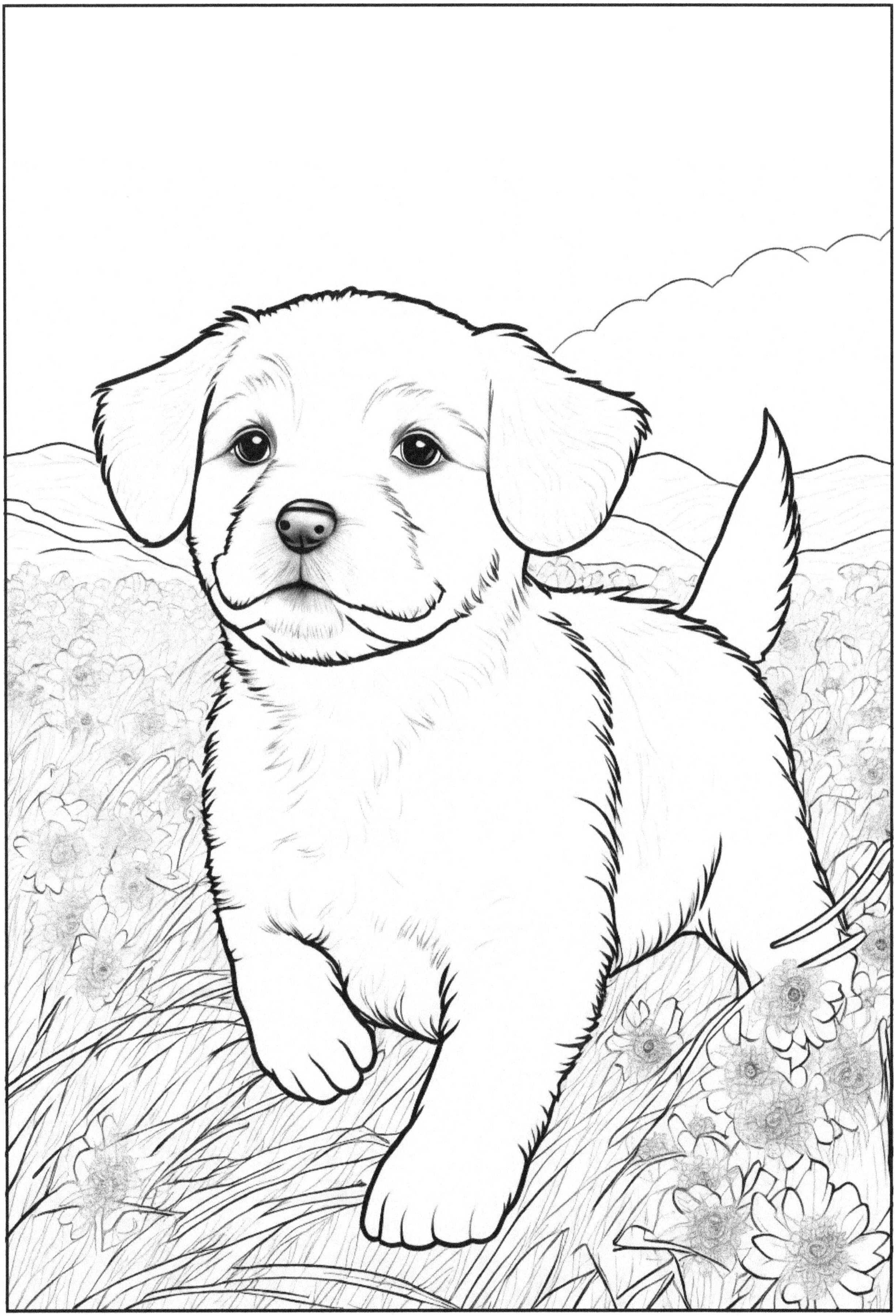

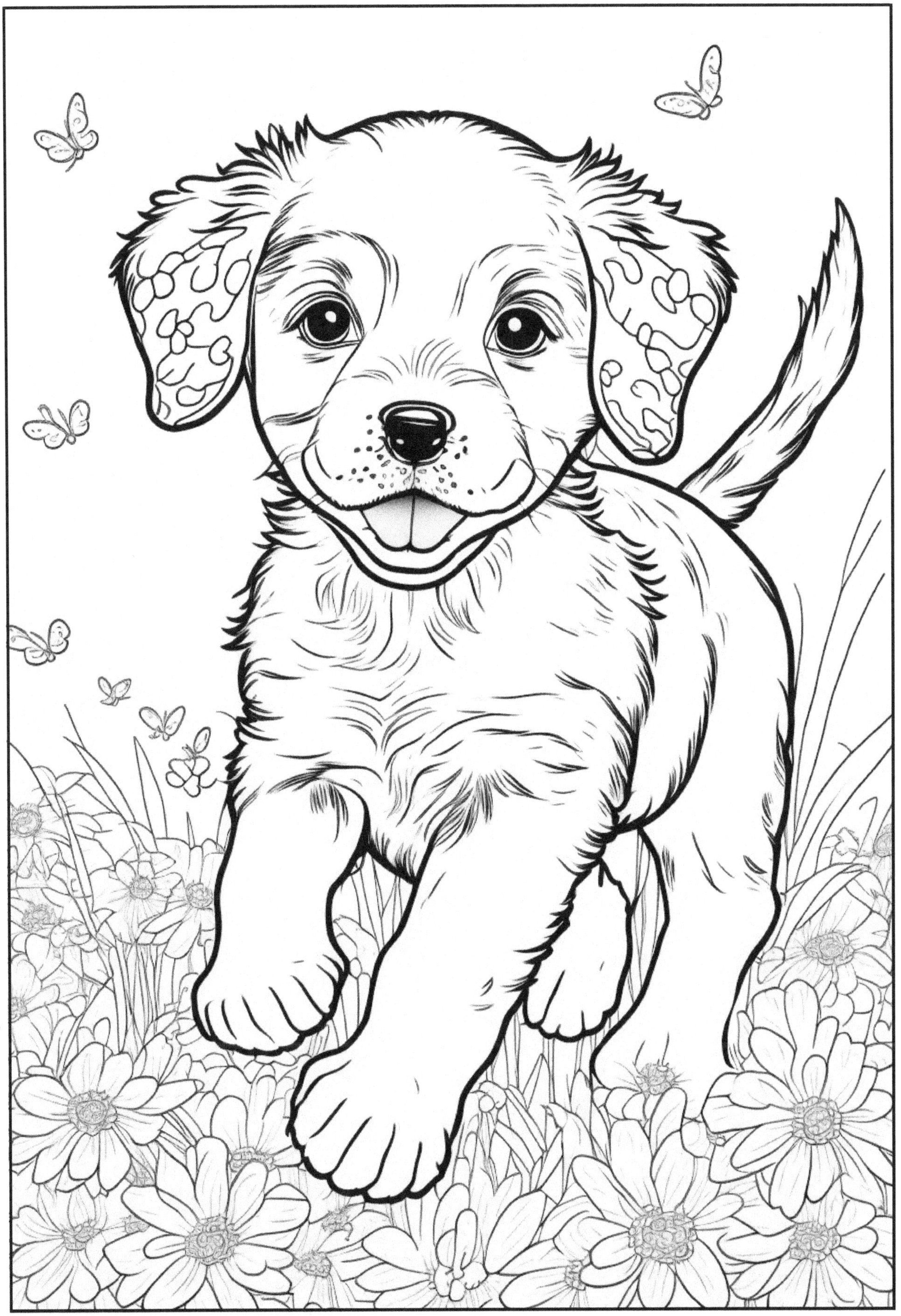

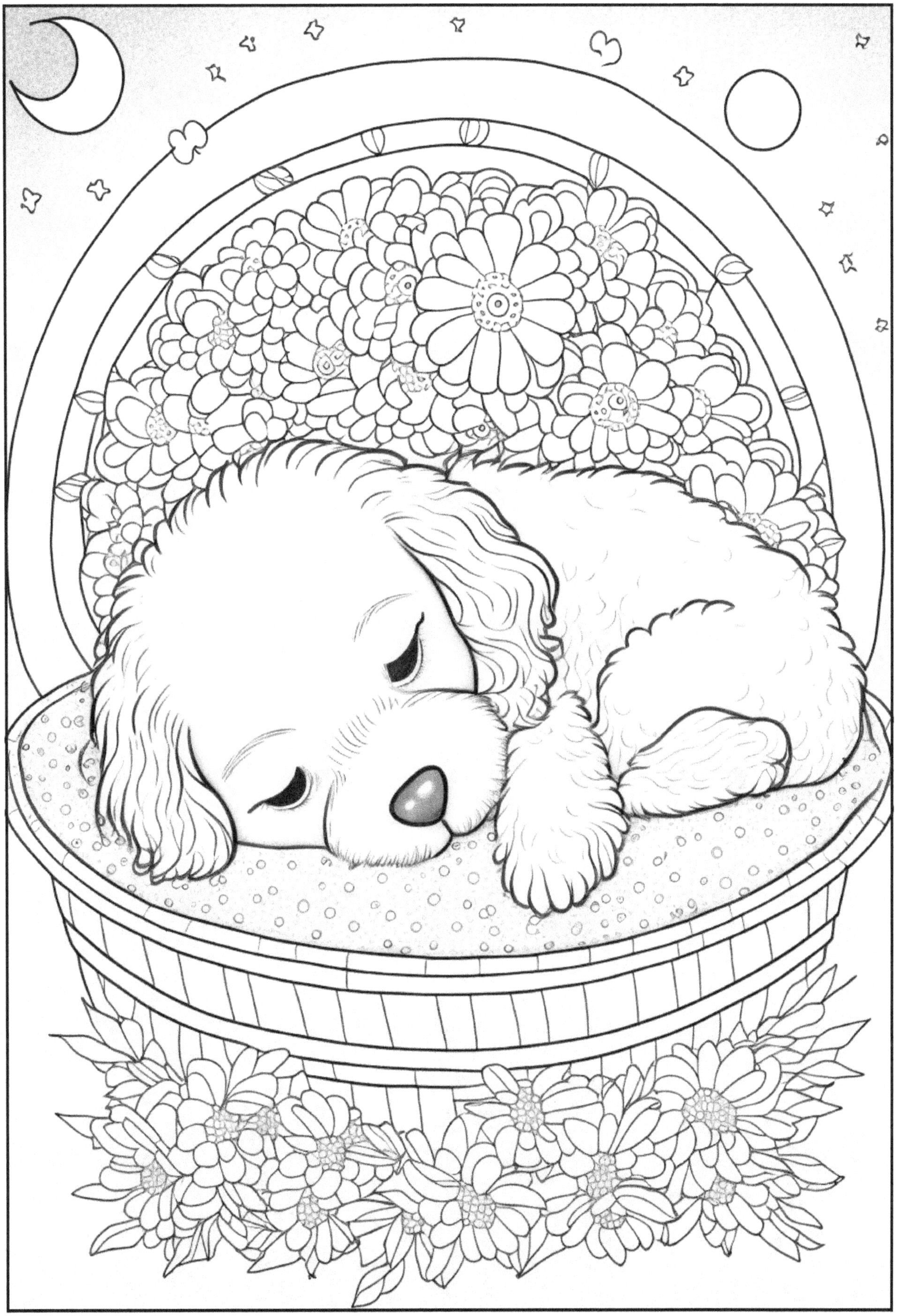

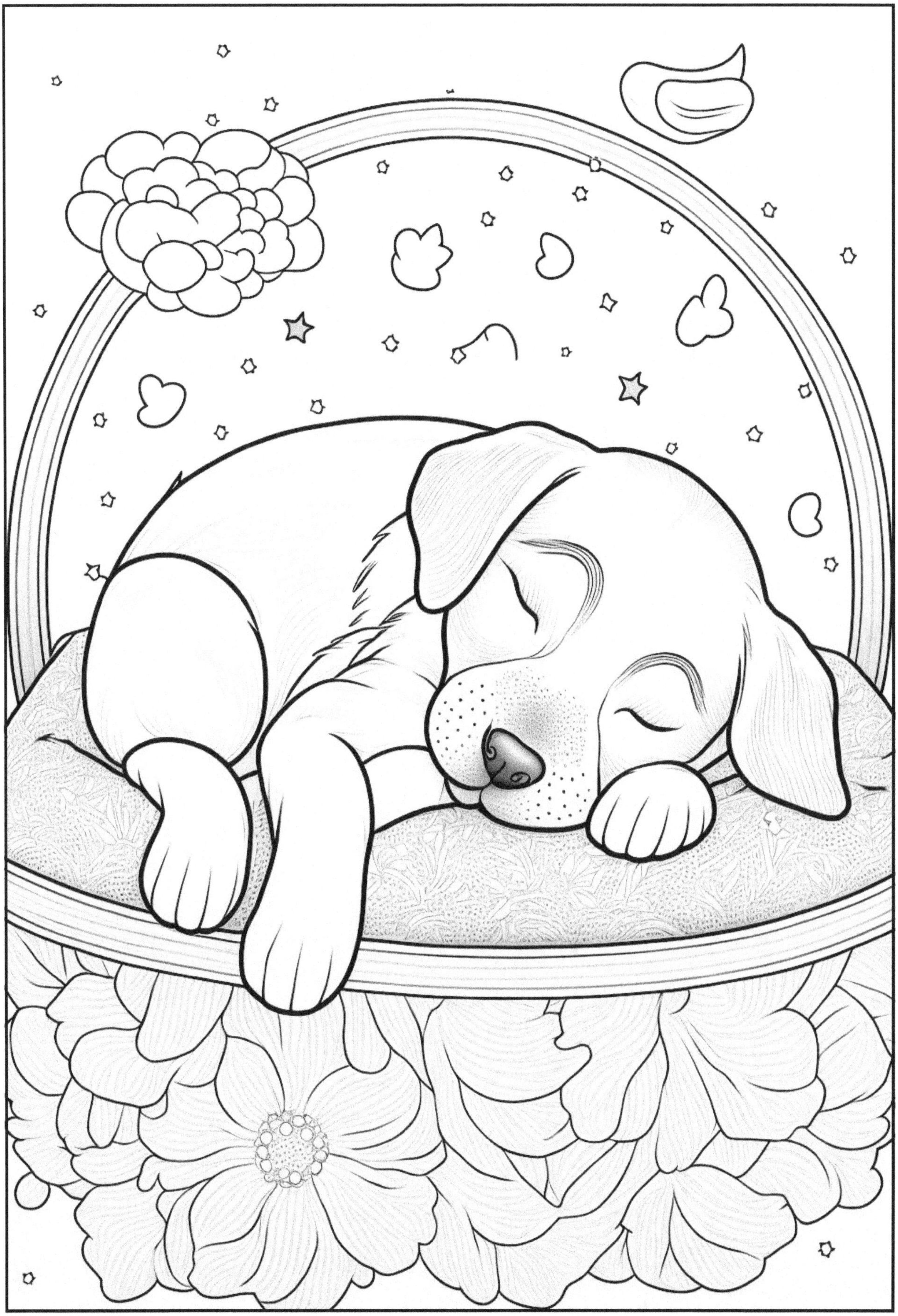

www.ingramcontent.com/pod-product-compliance
Lightning Source LLC
Chambersburg PA
CBHW082150230526
45467CB00043B/2733